Nothing
in New England
is New
the poet's experiences in New England, America

by Rick Lupert

Nothing in New England Is New

Copyright © 2013 by Rick Lupert
All rights reserved

Ain't Got No Press

Design, and Layout ~ Rick Lupert
Author Photo ~ Addie Lupert

"At Colby's Breakfast and Lunch" originally appeared in *The Bicycle Review* Issue # 20 (February, 2015 - www.thebicyclereview.net)

Thank you Addie, Brendan, Derrick, Bernie and Sara, Greg and Mary, John Grillo, Nathaniel Hawthorne, The Revolutionaries, The Patriots, The British, The Pilgrims, The Wampanoag, The Great Sachem and you.

No part of this book may be used or reproduced in any manner whatsoever without written permission from the author except in the case of brief quotations embodied in critical articles and reviews. For more information or to contact the author for any reason try:

(818) 904-1021

or

15522 Stagg Street
Van Nuys, CA 91406

or

Rick@PoetrySuperHighway.com

or

PoetrySuperHighway.com

First Edition ~ March, 2013

ISBN: 978-0-9820584-5-9 $13.00

Easy reading is damn hard writing.

- Nathaniel Hawthorne

The most serious charge which can be brought against New England is not Puritanism but February.

- Joseph Wood Krutch

The New England conscience ... does not stop you from doing what you shouldn't--it just stops you from enjoying it.

- Cleveland Amory

To Addie and everyone who fought to make America so I could wander around like an idiot making ridiculous observations.

On the Way

At LAX

If you are waiting in line at Burger King you are doing the wrong thing.

I've Been to Madison, Wisconsin

I have been in four airports today.
One more than I thought and the final one,
not the one I intended.

I can finally say I've been to Madison, Wisconsin.
I can finally tell Newark *surprise!*
There was the added benefit of

the extra couple of hours in Chicago.
O'Hare and I never get to spend much
time together, so that was nice.

I understand my luggage will be
going to Philadelphia. Good for it!
It's a wonderful city, rich in history

and brotherly love. I hope it gets to
see the Liberty Bell. Maybe get a
Philly Cheese Steak.

It's not a vegetarian
like us.

Unintentional Airports haiku

I
Oh O'Hare. Inside
you again. Part of the swarm.
The Tribune knows all.

II
Oh Madison. I
am finally inside you.
You know what I mean.

III
Oh Newark. Was born
somewhere near here. I think. Too
young to remember.

The Mile High Club

The turbulence somewhere over the United States of America has my son confident he's experiencing his first roller coaster. He is delighted. The rest of us on the plane would rather be on a roller coaster.

New Friend

The man in the seat next to me
who is not my wife, or my son
(thank you airline)
is taking up more seating space than
he has been allotted. Later I will send him a bill
for his knee and elbow incursions into my area.
I'm confident this can be resolved outside
the courts.

Nothing in New England is New

We are looking forward to traveling through New England, though I'm not sure how new it is as every attraction in the guidebook is described as "old."

Vigilant

They are preparing the cabin for landing.
The man next to me didn't turn off his cell phone. Just hid it under his leg. This is the same guy whose knee and elbow I mentioned earlier. So if you hear that my plane exploded, you'll know it was a victory for the personal space invading terrorists...
A sad day for America.

Power

There is only so much energy in my phone.
The Pilgrims never had to worry about this.

Location Is Everything

I am seated next to the bathroom door
in the very last row of the airplane.
The door doesn't quite shut all the way.
This is the greatest day of my life.

Homeland

It is ninety-two degrees in Newark, New Jersey.
Let's add *humid* and *cesspool* to the list of
words that describe this place.

Fondly Assessing the Situation

Oh the airports my luggage has seen.

Eastward

Bethlehem

I
We get in our rented Chrysler.
Chrysler. Which Addie says reminds her of Christ
which is great as we're heading to Bethlehem
where Christ was born. Sort of. And I think
Oh good we're getting all of our Christ mentions
out of the way early so all the Jews reading this
won't have to worry about it later.

II
We see a sign that says "Allentown. City of no limits."
Addie says "No limits? Come on Allentown! All you
did was put in a new frozen yogurt store. No limits indeed."

We drive to breakfast with Jesus.

III
We note everyone in the Blue Sky Cafe
in Bethlehem is young...the staff, the patrons.
It is before the after-church crowd so that
could change. We consider canceling our
vacation to do an ongoing demographic study
of the place. Instead we eat sweet potato quesadilla
drive to Springfield and wish them well.

Say this a Million Times Fast

We approach the town of Mahwah, New Jersey.
We wonder if they have a Wawa market there.
If they did, we could stop there, call people,
and tell them we're at the *Mahwah-Wawa*
which would surely delight all involved.

A Salute to the Past

for Fred Condo

While driving north on I-287 through New Jersey,
I remember Fred who now lives in San Francisco
and has chosen sides.

It was the era of the bottle cap when men were men
and women were women which I guess you could
say about any era if you think about it.

I was only seventeen then, and other people
were other ages which was fine and all part
of the natural order of things.

Fred once said, "today's cars are engineered
to get optimal fuel consumption at speeds much
higher than the posted speed limits."

He said this in an exasperated fashion as if
it was the most important thing in the world.
I think of this and wonder if I am getting

my money's worth in this mid-size rental car
as I drive the speed limit, not with fuel in mind
but, to avoid entrapment.

I only like to get tickets in the great state
of New York where my uncle the lawyer
can write a letter and make them go away.

I salute you Fred
from the other side of the country.
You have chosen well.

In Deference to the Previous Poem

Crossed the New York state line
and Addie shouts *book it!*

I love a good literary reference
when someone's asking me to break the law.

I see a sign that says

Vehicles with explosives must use next exit.

I guess New York is now relying
on the honor system for terrorists.

Canadian Hearing Society Revisited

I mumble inaudibly to Addie
We're passing the New York School For the Deaf.
What? She responds. And I repeat it louder,
my plan working perfectly unlike in Toronto
when a crazy person asked for directions
and ruined the whole thing.

Ongoing Illiteracy and a Horrible, Horrible Pun

I mis-read a sign that says *Shake Shack* as *Shame Shack*.
Either way it's a good place to take the kids.
I know, I know I should be ashaked of myself.

Addie Asks What the Plan Is

I say we'll have to play it by ear.
She doesn't hear me and says *what*
leaning in closer with her hand up to her ear.
So I say it again louder emphasizing the word *ear*
realizing the unintentional brilliance of this whole exchange.

Sign of the Apocalypse

I see a stretch limousine parked
at a McDonalds somewhere in Connecticut.
My God they should erase this whole state
and start over. They're just doing it wrong.

It Works!

I accidentally hit
the panic button
on the car key
and then completely
freak out.

Fourth Reich

When the people in the blue Toyota Rav 4
speed ahead not allowing us to merge
I naturally assume they are founding members
of the original NAZI party. After they're in front
of us and they toss cigarette butts out the window
it is confirmed.

Springfield

In the Springfield Museums

The bathrooms are
to the left of the polar bear.

For the love of God
you do not want to go

to the right
of the polar bear.

4 Odalisques by John Grillo

Addie delights in pointing out
the painting of naked women with cats.
She knows what I like.

Addie Likes That the Bechetold Water Colors are all Untitled

Lets your imagination run wild, she says
I have decided that they're all called
Herbert the Magic Watercolor.

A Japanese Corner by John Haberle, 1898

One artist has painted the words *do not touch* into his painting which has saved the museum a bundle on paying a guy to stand in the room and say that all day.

Last Judgement by Jan Mandyn, 1550

One painting has Jesus sitting on an orb
kind of like a Death Star, passing final judgement
on all the characters below.

I think I see Luke Skywalker's foreskin
in the lower right hand corner.

Word Nook

One display in the Springfield History Museum
is a little cubby you get inside where a recording
tells you language puzzles. It's called the Word Nook.

I pass by it hoping there's a Bad Word Nook
in the next room.

Downtown Springfield is the Deadest Place I've Seen

Twenty-six blocks and the only sign of life
is one guy and his dog on Chestnut Street.
We pass by a store called Chestnut Packages.
but this town is so dead I don't even want to say
something funny about that. My wife laughs anyway.
Sometimes that's all I need. We get on the highway
for the coast. Leave this deadness behind.

Destiny Discovery

I see a billboard that reads
Your car has enemies, Rick is the ally.

Up 'til now I've only been there for kittens.
Looks like I'm being forced to branch out.

Thought on the Massachusetts Turnpike

I
A sign says *Plows Use Caution*.
I don't know if this is an instruction to plows that
they should use caution, or a warning to me that
plows are up ahead and that I should use caution
or an informational message letting everyone
know that plows use caution. I just know that
it's eighty-four degrees and I haven't seen a plow
since 1982.

II
A sign on the highway advises *reduced salt area ahead*.
This is where my cardiologist wanted me to vacation.

III
I'm pretty sure that the symbol for the Massachusetts Turnpike
is not an Amish Hat*, but it sure looks like one. On behalf of the
non-driving Amish civilization who, for the purposes of this poem,
I now claim to represent I would like to express our outrage.

IV
We drive by Walden Pond without stopping because
we wish to get to our destination deliberately.

* *It was probably a Pilgrim's hat.*

Sight Seeing

One of the highway 495 signs is so large
it causes Addie to say *What is this the road for the blind?*
After one hundred years of laughter I tell her *no honey
if this were the road for the blind the signs would be in braille.*

Portsmouth

At Colby's Breakfast and Lunch

I
The sign in the door says *No Politicians, No Exceptions*.
So I am here to report, America, that my only agenda
is to put coffee inside of me. My pledge to you, citizens
of New England, if you bring me eggs and *anadama* bread
I will put it directly in my mouth for the betterment of all.
My fellow morning diners, let me into your kitchen and
I will give you my credit card, as long as you promise
to give it back after conducting the transaction which
pays for my meal. The future is ours, Portsmouth.
God bless you, your mighty coconut, pancakes,
your vegetarian sausage. We're taking back breakfast,
one vittle at a time.

II
Colby's is slanted.
You feel at any moment you
and your breakfast might slide out
the front door onto Daniel Street.

III
Another sign says *No cell phones, be polite*.
I try to explain to the waiter I am just writing poetry.
He says it's okay and tells us the story of the fist fight that
occurred when one patron was furious at a loud woman
on her phone at a different table. He doesn't like it when
he sees a table full of people not looking at each other.
I spend the rest of the meal staring into Addie's eyes
and hoping to God I can make the coffee into my mouth
without looking.

IV
You can tell the tourists, like us,
all who head to the front door
only to see the sign *Please use Side Door.*
The quick turnaround shuffle to the side entrance
a dance the locals never do.

V
Andrew tells us the story of *Anadama Bread*
A fisherman came home, frustrated with the
mush his wife, Anna, had made, made a dough
out of it with flour and molasses. While it baked
he sat by the fire muttering *Anna, damn her.*
Anna, damn her. The bread was so delicious
the neighbors baked it too, and then all of
New England. From hated mush to beloved bread,
Anna should be praised for the inspiration.

VI
Do I pay here or at the counter I ask Andrew
However you want, he says, *It's just me and Julie.*
So anything goes? I ask.
Anything goes. he answers.

Strawbery Banke

The Chase Family

The Chase family who hosted Washington
had lead plates before congress outlawed them,
had a tea table, duplicated here in their house.

The original in a museum in Pittsburgh.
A switch would be complicated.
Charles tells us museums prefer to

amass antiquities as opposed to disperse them.
The Chases donated their home to the city
for use as an orphanage, Charles tells us.

He is from Sicily, prefers not to take
compliments. My family is from Sicily
and I just eat that stuff up.

The Aldrich House

Home of Thomas Bailey Aldrich
poet and one time editor of *The Atlantic Monthly*.
Friend to Mark Twain, Louisa May Alcott, Henry Pierce
wrote the loosely autobiographical *The Story of the Bad Boy*.
We don't judge him for this.

In the Shapiro House

I
The table is still set for *Shabbes* dinner.
Addie remarks the chicken doesn't look so appetizing.
I tell her this is one of the original cooked chickens from 1909.
She now feels better about the display chicken.

II
There is a picture of an unidentified
orthodox Jewish boy.
The year is 1910.
He looks like he is on a cell phone.
We are an advanced people.

III
We spend more time in the Shapiro house than
anywhere else at Strawbery Banke.
Partially because we feel connected and mostly
because the period dressed actress stationed there
found out we were Jewish and wanted to tell us everything
she knew. She wanted to make sure we were warm
had a place for dinner, were happily married,
making little Jewish babies. After several hours
of information, and thirty more buildings to see
she lets us go. We will always have a home in Puddledock.

Where the Children Play

Addie walks into *Children's Discovery Center*
where we can take our children if they get antsy.
The woman inside looks at my adult wife and says
"You know this is the children's building don't you?"
Clearly she has not met my wife, child at heart,
in her antsy phase.

Another Shapiro Sighting

Mrs. Shapiro spots us outside of Pitt Tavern
and tells us this is where thirsty people would
make a Pitt Stop, then laughs maniacally and
walks back to her house.

Addie says she is sick of smiling at all these people
She wants to be nice but her face is starting to hurt.

How to Know If You Can Go In

They put an American flag up in front of the
buildings you are allowed to enter. I will adopt
this system as my own and will now feel free to walk
into any house in Los Angeles displaying a flag
and demand an informative demonstration.

Nomenclature

Strawbery Banke changed its name to Portsmouth
in 1653 believing the name more befitting of a
great seaport. The discovered banks of wild
strawberries in 1630 a twenty year memory.

The cats name was J.D.

The black cat on the second floor
of the Sherburne house
has been waiting for me to pet her
since 1695

In the Gift Shop

I see a book called *The Poems of Abraham Lincoln*.
So I got to thinking. *Gettysburg Address*
Abraham Lincoln, slam poet!
I wonder if his beard counted as a prop.

Jewnity

In Portsmouth *Temple of Israel*
was the only synagogue in the united states
where Russian Jews and German Jews would pray together.
It reminds me of the story
of the Jew stranded on a desert island
who builds two synagogues.
When rescued and asked why he points to one
and says *this is the one I attend and
I would never set foot in that one.*
We have our peculiar ways but the
disparate Jews of Portsmouth,
Puddle Dock, held hands and
took a step forward.

Dishonest Vegetable

We walked by *Me and Ollie's Honest Foods*
where I'm pretty sure that an eggplant lied to me.

haiku

Does every city
in the world plan their trash nights
for our vacations?

Perfect!

It's kind of funny
that a couple spilled
a crate of strawberries
all over the lobby floor
of a hotel
in a town
that used to be called
Strawbery Banke

Moon

An intoxicated man stops directly in front of
where we are sitting at the intersection of Ceres
and Hanover. He has long, curly, dirty blonde hair
like a Robert Plant gone wrong. He realizes he is
standing directly in front of where we are sitting,
close enough to question his concept of personal space.
He decides to bring me in to his world and asks
"Do you think it's a full moon tonight" staring directly over
my head. "It's hard for me to say from this angle"
I respond as I am facing the other direction.
He laughs like a drunk man should.
I tell him the moon is always full, it's just not all visible.
I appear to have rocked his world like a Led Zeppelin.
"That's a good one" he said. No that was perfect.
We both move on with our evening.

Beers

We have a beer sampler with eight beers
"Which ones do you like" Addie asks
But by this point I have had too many
I tell her "I like the Wild Thang and the grapefruit
and" catching her eyes "I like you."
It could be romantic but I am intoxicated.
Addie tells me she is not a beer.
Still...and the rest of this poem
has been censored as I
imagine the possibilities.

They are Sweet Here

I am what feels like seventeen beers into the
eight beer sampler and the bartender is the same one
as last night. To us this is a novelty but to him
it is every day. Beverages for the thirsty,
tourists and locals alike. We are the former and will
leave this place tomorrow. And don't we all want them
to treat us as locals. Like we have the inside track.
Know which door to enter the breakfast place.
Don't bother ordering the beer sampler because we
know them all and can spread it out over our entire lives.
The red ale has a sweetness to it. It's not our favorite
but it is like the people in Portsmouth. Sweet. We like them.
We like their stouts and ales. Their dirty blondes.
We finish all the beers in the sampler.
It is only a taste.

Context

A family getting into the hotel elevator
tell their little boy "number two." I'm sure
they're referring to what button he should press
but being in the middle of potty training I can
only hope he doesn't take a shit in the middle
of the elevator floor.

An American French Toast Story

Addie is devastated she didn't even touch
the second piece of French toast at *The Friendly Toast*.
To be fair they were larger than her head but she hates
to waste food. I try to make her feel better by telling her
it's not a big deal, put it into perspective and think
about those poor people who were burned at the stake
in Salem, Massachusetts, whose graves we will visit in
just a couple of hours. Well, she's forgotten about the
French toast anyway.

Salem

Driving the East Coast

is miles of highway surrounded by forests
unlike in Los Angeles where the forests
have all run away from the freeways
like frightened little dogs

We Pass by the Century House Restaurant in Peabody, Massachusetts

Their sign advertises
Unexcelled Food

which I think means their food
isn't very good.

It's okay Century House Restaurant,
your food can excel

if you apply yourself.

The Entrance to one Cemetery is on Grover Street

It makes me wonder if muppets are buried there.

In the Nathaniel Hawthorne House

Family Portrait

His children, Julian and Rose, all look pissed
as any kids would who were made to dress up
and sit for a photograph.

Moved

This isn't the original location of the house.
It was moved here. So although he was born here.
he wasn't born here.

Things

His house is filled with mundane possessions.
Like the chess board he used with Julian and Rose.
I can't wait until I die and they turn my house into a museum
My collection of Simpsons DVDs, my stockpile of cat hair.
They'll call it the *Rick Lupert Museum and Birth Place*.
I wasn't born there, but I still want them to call it that.

In the House of the Seven Gables

I
They claim to have a secret staircase.
But they advertise it in the brochure
so that's kind of dumb.

II
Here in front of one of the oldest houses in America
We hear a woman's cell phone emit "DROID."
Ah the sounds of the past come alive I tell Addie.
She's too tired to walk away so she just turns her
head and takes a deep breath.

III
Everyone knows about the secret staircase.
They might as well call it the staircase
that everyone knows about.

IV
They tell us to watch our heads because of the low doorways
and we laugh our little heads off with our tiny squeaky voices
like the little mouse people we are.

V
The fireback in the great chamber is engraved
with the words "an ape can never be a man."

Clearly the authors of the book of Genesis
where this quote comes from never saw

Any Which Way You Can
starring clint Eastwood and an orangutan named Clyde

who was more of a man
then I'll ever be.

You Probably Don't Need Context for This

Addie does a little foot jig to mock me which I deserve for some reason.

The Goths are Out in Salem

Pierced noses, pale skin
black *Skinny Puppy* tee-shirts.
Witchcraft! Burned at the stake?
Fuck yeah! Let's make a day of it!

Any Which Way You Can

A group of costumed performers regale us
with *the news of the day* in downtown Salem.
Also present is a man dressed as a pirate, full regalia.
He is not part of the group of costumed actors.
This is just how he chose to dress up in Salem today.

One Store in Salem Sells a Potato Ricer

It seems you can combine any two things
and have another thing. Potato Ricer
Melon Appler. Spoon Forker. I could go on.
No wait, Addie has forbidden me to go on.

The Men's Bathroom in the Salem Mall is Not Labeled

That's how they tell if you are a witch,
if you know to go inside.

P.S. It *does* smell like witchery inside.

I mean *pee* s.

Fell in a Hole

When our tour guide tells us the story of how she fell in a hole
we laugh, not because we aren't sympathetic to what happened to her,
but because it's funny when somebody says they fell in a hole.

Searching for Witches

> *It were better that ten suspected witches should escape,*
> *than that the innocent person should be condemned.*
> ~ Increase Mathers, 1693

A thick red line takes us to all the hot spots
the fake museums. The old well. The cemeteries

with crypts collapsing. A human guide tells us how it is.
She tells us what it means to be pressed.

They'd lay you on the ground. A board on top of you.
A stone placed on the board. If you didn't confess

they'd put on another stone.
until you were dead. Pressed.

We sit near the marker for Sarah Wildes
Hanged July 19, 1692.

It took until 1992 for the town of Salem
to make a memorial to their *witches*.

On Halloween, our guide tells us,
it's like Mardi Gras here.

Some Wiccans come to the memorial,
bow down to the ground and claim

they feel the energy of their ancestors.
Our guide wants to tell them they weren't

witches. They miss the point of the memorial
It is not a celebration of the occult.

It is how Germany feels about World War II
It is an embarrassment.

Boston

Noise at Night

The midnight explosions
across the street from
our hotel can be attributed
to Fourth of July revelry
and not to the complete
destruction of the
Boston Public Library.
One can hope.

On the Freedom Trail

We stop by Paul Revere's house.
He is not home.

The Sole of My Sneaker Came Off Last Night

And by *sole* I mean a crisis that can be solved by super glue and not the hiring of an exorcist.

I guess if you're reading this on the page you already figured that out.

haiku

The T creaks like Tin
Man when first met Dorothy
Oil can oil can.

At Anthem Kitchen and Bistro, Fenueil Hall

I
The coffee is not strong.
A sugar cube could take it.

Put in milk and it's like you're drinking
milk.

This is New England people. Your coffee
fueled a revolution. This coffee is barely

one guy in the back of the room with
his hand raised meekly saying *excuse me.*

This is the coffee the British would serve
to their enemies. Our waiter apologizes

Explains to us about packets and water ratios.
Brings us a tea box.

I remember something about tea and this city.

I choose one called *Awake*.
It will do its job until later

when the brewery tour
will put me to sleep.

II

One of the waiters here nervously removes
the coffee cups from the tables.

Says they give him anxiety.
He didn't get a job at a bar to serve breakfast.

He wants lunch here faster
than a Paul Revere.

Benedicts make him uncomfortable
for the obvious reasons.

III

Addie is in love with her breakfast.
I wonder if she will be thinking of it

later tonight
when the fireworks go off.

Does anybody really want to hear a poem equating what I'm doing in the bathroom at Faneuil Hall with the American Revolution?

No.

At Old Granary Burial Point

I
People put pennies on Josiah and Abiah Franklin's headstones.
The last thing these people need is money I think.
They gave the world Benjamin Franklin,
were married fifty five years.
They have everything they need.

II
At Paul Revere's grave
I want to tell him
You were right.
They came.

Life Imitates Filmed Art

A stranger at the downtown crossing T station
gets off an orange line train wearing a shirt that says
I know your secret. She is probably sixteen years old.
I put on my wild eyes and ask *Do you know my secret?*
I try to salivate or froth at the mouth.
I don't really have a secret, but now she thinks I do.
I just wanted to have a moment like in the movies.

Mystery

If you read page 13 of *A Man With No Teeth Serves Us Breakfast* or page 17 of *Death of a Mauve Bat*, then you know exactly what I'm wearing under my pants.

Did He Ever Return?

I saw Charlie on the train.
He looked hungry and old.

I gave him a nickel
to end this madness.

In the Samuel Adams Brewery Tour

I
When the tour guide uses the phrase
Dry Hopping everyone on the tour giggles.

II
After the tour and tasting
ahhahaaahhahaahhahhaaaa
who the flerck knows?

Weather or Not

The problem with wearing my American flag red white and blue striped underwear on the fourth of July (did you really think I'd leave you hanging page 90?) is that they are knit and not the best choice for eighty degree Boston weather, with sixty percent humidity. But I am a patriot so here we are.

California is Cancelled

They put free lollipops
in the bathroom of our hotel
so pretty much we want to live here
for the rest of our lives.

Art Walk

We stop in an art gallery on Newbury Street
partially because the chalkboard in front

of the store has impressive names on it
and mostly because they have air conditioning.

It is a small crowd on Independence Day
so they have the classic rock station on

We are looking at Chagall, Warhol and Dali
accompanied by a symphony of Osborne.

There is no place in the world this
wouldn't make sense to me.

There is a Store Here Called Grab and Go

They forgot to put *and Pay* in the name.
It's causing a problem.

Quick Smackdown

I see the book
Paris Versus New York
in Trident Booksellers.

I don't have a lot of time
so I skip to the last page
to see who won.

Food Coma

After the fried goat cheese with honey and sweet onion
Queso con Miel at *Tapeo* on Newbury Street I go into a food coma.
I throw a conniption on the ground. I froth at the mouth.
My eyes roll back into my head (where else would they go?)
The waitress asks if everything is okay. I ask if they
are insured for food comas. She says *no* but wishes
they were because she is in one now. I drink more
sangria and stumble out to wherever it is we are going.

Waiting for the Sky to Explode

They shut down the highway next to the Charles River
so people like me can sit on it and watch the fireworks.

It's much nicer to sit here tonight than to be stuck here
in a car like last night when an hour of our lives was sucked away.

Fireworks start in an hour and forty minutes
so we have plenty of time to reassess everything.

Our lives, our relationship, how it is to spend a week
without our son and why it is that my phone is still

searching for a signal while Addie's seems to be in cahoots
with the wireless company. I'd tell you their name but

I don't think they deserve it and I refuse to accept
product placement deals in my poetry. By the way

Have you been to Mulberry Street Pizza in Sherman Oaks?
It's really great. Soon the barges will shoot lights in the sky.

Despite it being an hour and a half away it is so little time
in the grander scheme of things. Soon this entire week

of days will be a distant memory and we'll be struggling
to remember the smallest details of this experience.

So better to remember them now...while they're happening.
The Boston Pops is playing the *Raiders of the Lost Ark*

theme in tribute to John Williams' eightieth birthday.
Here with my wife on the highway, I've never felt more alive.

A Poem with the Word Fireworks in it Four Times, the Word Rain Three Times, That Ends with the Word Awesome.

They delayed the start of the fireworks
for the rain that didn't come. They started
the fireworks and then the rain came.
It became more intense as the fireworks did.
When the fireworks ended, the rain ended.
It was awesome.

Knowing the Signs

I discover in the hotel bathroom
a container Addie has labeled
Kinky Curly Curling Custard
It's gong to be an amazing evening.

Skilled Labor

I ordered the *build your own omelette*
They brought me three raw eggs, a
frying pan, a tool belt and asked if
I was a part of the union.

Addie Says the Cell Phone Strap is Annoying

Not as annoying as hurling your phone into the Charles River I respond.
Score one for Rick Lupert!
(Addie's score is 973)

Again on Newbury Street

We pass by *The Fairy Store* at which point
I launch into an overly dramatic diatribe
about fairies which would best not be described here.

Important Decision

I decide that tickets for the T should be called *Teekets*.

That's it really.

Advanced Preparation

I tell Addie
in the most serious manner I can muster
that the museum closes at 9:45 pm.
So no dilly dallying. The time now:
Twelve noon.

Make Your Own Kind of Music

Periodically the subway goes above ground.
It is at these times I get everybody's attention
on the train and tell them this should now
be called the *supraway*.

This will be the last time I'm allowed
in Boston.

I Can't Read

I see a sign which reads *Gardner Museum Simmons College*
which I think says *Gene Simmons College*

I wonder if either are related to Richard and if
they take transfer credits from the university of life.

MFA

At the Museum

I
It costs twenty-seven dollars to valet park
your car at the Museum of Fine Arts in Boston.
Remind me to never drive my car here
from Los Angeles.

II
Addie misreads the Coat Check sign as
    Goat Check.
It would have been nice.

III
There are foreigners here.
Either that or that is the language
indigenous to the MFA bathroom
and I am *l'etranger*.

IV
Addie has a fight with the bathroom sink.
She describes the altercation.
Apparently the sink won.
She refuses to tell me who started it.

V
Old photography captures
images of people alive
long before anyone today
took a breath.
Captured alive.
Forever alive.

Paper Zoo

I
I'm sure Picasso's *The Toad* (1949)
is as attractive to other toads
as his women are to us.

II
Strutting Bird
Berthold Löffler 1903

Now I know where Travolta
got his inspiration.

III
Honolulu Hawaii (Peacock)
Lee Friedlander 1977

To take a picture of a peacock
in black and white
leaves a lot to the imagination
which, perhaps
is the point.

IV
A Lion Emerging From a Cave
James Darnell 1792

He looks pissed.

V
Trout and Reflection
Neil Welliver 1980

    For Brautigan

I have nothing to say
about this etching
except it is, in fact, trout.

Musical Instruments

I
Harp Guitar
Larson brothers 1920
Double necked, Half guitar, Half harp

I can see Jimmy Page
rocking the fuck out of that.

II
Keyed Trumpet 1843
Leonardo Massarenti and Fratelli

We see an early trumpet.
How early? About 6 am.

III
There were concerns the eerie sound the musical glasses
would make by rubbing moistened fingers along the rims
was causing insanity in the 1740's among listeners and players.
Kind of like popular music today.

Ekphrastia

I
Amber Jewel Casket
Fritz Von Miller 1880-85

I want to grab the jewel casket out of the jewelry room
so I can get two energy points in *Adventure World*.
The museum staff, Addie, the people of Boston
and probably everyone I know would prefer that I not.

II
Addie calls one sarcophagus the *Boob Tomb*
because of its boob like protrusions.
Maybe we should call women boob people.

III
The Egyptian statue of the goddess Sekhmet
has the body of a woman and the head of a cat.
Finally all of my loves in one perfect package.

Note to my wife in the event she reads this:
Just kidding. You are the perfect package.

IV
Don't you think its ironic that
in the room *Conservation in Action*
nothing is happening. Addie points out the
Back after lunch sign which is not at all the point.

V
The Massachusetts College of Art and Design
used to be called *The Massachusetts Normal Art School*
back when such a thing existed.

VI
Self Portrait
William Merritt Chase, 1884
American Impressionism, pastel on canvas

Imagine trying to maintain a pose
while simultaneously painting yourself.

VII
The Woman in the Yellow Room
Frederick Carl Frieseke, 1910

She's how I imagine you, Elizabeth.
Only the finest things
A kimono, remarkable shoes.
Fuzzy like your eyes which
see the entire world as
impressions.

VIII
Mother and Child in a Boat
Edmund Tarbell 1892

I like how the reflection and light on the water
matches that of the woman's dress
Addie says.

I like the way the child's eyes
make it look like she's the Anti-Christ
Rick says.

IX
Today our son in Allentown
is with his grandparents at the *Touch Museum*.
Addie asks if there is anything she can touch here.
Not while anyone is looking I tell her.

X
Addie wonders why they bother
putting noses on the statues if
they're just going to always fall off.
I really am going to give her
an author's credit this time.

XI
You can walk around the museum with dogs
but not with a backpack on both shoulders
according to the docent woman who has
clearly lived a long enough life to be able
to tell us these things. Addie puts the other strap
back on when we leave the gallery she is monitoring
like tea tossed in the harbor.

XII
I know exactly where the Asian man wearing
neon green sneakers is, so I guess they are working.

XIII
Åse #7 Pot
Arne Åse 1933

Addie calls it *cup and blade*.
I call it *cut your face open coffee mug*.

XIV
A couple of doors lean up against the wall in the
Contemporary Art Gallery. Like they were left there
by accident when the exhibit was created and
they didn't realize it until after opening day so
they just put up a plaque.

XV
Modern video art
with its strobe and quick
repeating images

Addie thinks they should
warn you before you come in
that you might seize

Death of a Mauve Bat

When the angry woman on the T yells
Shut the Fuck Up!
I want to tell her *yeah I love that video!*
I don't think she'd get my *General Idea*.

Boston, Still

Bell In Hand

I am in one of the oldest pubs in the United States
drinking beer you can only get in this manner in this place.

They have fireman urinals in the bathroom.
I didn't know the founding fathers were so tall.

A sailor and his friend walk in and remark on
the small size of the room. They have to shimmy

around me to get to the facilities. I say *yes it is
a small bathroom but it is nice to meet you both.*

They have *wifi* here now. Something the patriots
never would have imagined. Revere could have

just texted his message. The tavern sits
across the street from the Holocaust memorial.

The Freedom Trail is inclusive. We have seen it before,
the memorial, and don't want to wander through after beer.

So we will drink up, make our way to the Old North Church
let them tell us what they have to tell us.

The trail to freedom begins with *Bell in Hand Ale*
and root fries, three kinds, Idaho, sweet potato

and waffle. America has come
so far.

Is this the end of the Freedom Trail?

the boy asks in front of the locked gate
at Old North Church. It is closed early
for a wedding rehearsal.

There'll be no more freedom today boy.
Get to shoveling my nicky-nackies
and peel my onions for dindin.

He scurries away hoping for freedom
on the morrow.

Unfortunate Hats

Three teenaged girls walk on Hanover Street
wearing tall white paper hats which, from behind,
make them look like they're members of the Ku Klux Klan.
Rich in Jewish and Italian History, Boston's North End
a melting pot for all.

Trash Night in Boston

Wonderful.
Wonderful.

I'd Do It My Way

If I ran the restaurant *Marco* on Hanover Street,
when the phone rang I would answer "Marco?"
and if they didn't Respond "Polo" I would interrupt
them and say "I'm sorry that's not correct"
and then hang up.

While Waiting for Something to Happen

Addie refers to the *Crayola Factory*
But it sounds like *Gorilla Factory*.
I'd rather go to the Gorilla Factory.

Oh My God

The truffle oil infused mushroom risotto at *Marco* on Hanover Street is exactly what the founding fathers had in mind when they came up with America.

Goodbye Boston

I'm writing to you from the rental car on route to Plymouth
which sound unsafe, but technology and an extra set of hands
make it okay.

The boys and girls on the college radio station are playing
the music that hasn't been invented yet, with exception,
The Replacements, *Beer for Breakfast*.

It sounds like a good idea but I have already drank the ale of the patriots
And there's an omelet awaiting me twenty miles ahead in Plymouth,
home of the famous rock.

There are no signs on the highway stating the speed limit,
so I guess it's up to me. This is what it means
to be American.

Plymouth

Massachusetts has Thought of Everything

The sign on Route 3 south says
Traveling Prohibited in Breakdown Lane
which is thoughtful as those people
have it bad enough

haiku

Tonight we will sleep
in Providence where they set
the river on fire

Plymouth Rock

I
Plymouth rock is not the biggest rock.
But don't feel bad. It makes more money
than the other rocks.

II
Plymouth rock is not the biggest rock.
But don't feel bad. No other rocks
get asked for their autograph.

III
I saw Plymouth Rock at the Playboy Mansion
nestled between two bunnies who were telling it
their life story. Plymouth Rock nodded as they spoke
like a wise old Pilgrim.

IV
Everyone wondered what I was doing
at the Playboy Mansion.

Persy's Place, Downtown Plymouth

I
They offer *Endless Eggs.*

I'm still eating them.

II
A man with no teeth serves us breakfast.
It looks like he just stepped off the Mayflower.

III
The menu is so large it can only be viewed in its entirety
from outer space. We don't have that kind of time, or
the resources so we just order from our memory of
what breakfast foods exist.

IV
The staff here is so young
after the waiter brings us our food
we have to change his diaper.

V
The coffee here is passable.
But barely. Addie says it is not send-backable
and that's enough for me.

Wampanoag

On Thanksgiving day Native Americans gather
on Cole's Hill in Plymouth. To them it is a day of mourning.
They consider Thanksgiving to be a genocide.

Statue

I take a close up picture
looking up to the face of
Great Sachem.

Addie sees me
and says I could call this book
Up Great Sachem's Loin Cloth.

At the Rock

Plymouth Rock broke twice when they tried to
move it to *protect* it. Now they leave it where it is
and it stays in one piece.

The Pilgrims never mentioned the rock.
But the park ranger says it was reasonable.
We don't have rocks where we come from I tell her.
That's a lie Addie chimes in.

At the Mayflower II

The bone player walks off the Mayflower II and
into the men's bathrooms which smells like
it hasn't been cleaned since 1620. Then he exits
and walks into modern Plymouth in full period costume.
I'd imagine they are used to this kind of thing.

Near Plymouth Rock is Pebbles Restaurant

This explains why the rock keeps getting smaller.

Misunderstanding

One store in Plymouth has a sign which says *Ask about enlargements.* I go in, have a conversation and am quickly ushered out.

Pilgrim Hall Museum

I
We are thrilled to no end that
the piece of Plymouth rock here
says *Please Touch*.

We cancel the rest of our trip
with plans to spend the rest of our time,
hands caressing this historic beauty.
We may not return home.

II
*I caress the Plymouth Rock fragment and
feel the energy of the pilgrims who trod upon it*
is probably how the false witches of modern Salem
would describe this experience.

III
We keep traveling back in time on these trips
like a few years ago when we started in revolutionary Boston
and then went to King George the III in England.
We started in colonial Boston on this trip and now find
ourselves in seventeenth century Plymouth.
If we go any further we might see dinosaurs.

IV
Addie makes a rubbing
in Pilgrim Hall museum
because she can.

V
Judging by the printing in these old books
and the engravings on old library buildings
the letter 'U' didn't get invented until 1923.

VI
A sign in front of Pilgrim Hall Museum says
Treasure hunt today. In the museum we can't find
the treasure hunt. Finding the treasure hunt is
the first part of the treasure hunt.

A Surfboard Shop
In the Middle of Plymouth

You know Miles Standish
ripped that shit.

They've Got an Oysteria Here

Seems like you can add *eria* to the end of any word
and have yourselves a legitimate thing.
Later tonight I'm going to a beereria.

Semantics

Every time we return to the rental car
Addie says she would like to get in the trunk.
She knows I know what she means, but she
also knows what I want it to mean.

A Sign on Sandwich Street says Blind Drive

Here a thousand American Stevie Wonders
have traveled to and fro for their lunch.

We Pass by the Plymouth Cat Clinic

I ask Addie is she thinks they would like me
to come in and pet all the cats.
She assures me it would be a good idea.

I Assume

in one of the smaller huts in the Wampanoag village that has a curtain at the door is where they used to have Wampanookie.

Addie asks if there's somewhere she can Wampapee.

Bulgarian Teenage Tourists In the Plimoth Plantation Gift Shop

It seems important.

Providence

At Food Restaurant on Empire Street (AS220)

Painted on a white wall with no windows are the words
Open Window. Just below, written on a chalk board
are the words "Poetry Slam 8:00. $4.00"
As soon as they see me, they erase the chalk board
and write "Dance Party 8:30. $6.00"
I'm not still thinking *Open Window*.

Providence

In Providence everyone looks like they are from
Portland or Seattle or, for all I know, Providence.

Flip flops and beards, even the women.
Everything is covered in art, especially the people.

It coats their skin and comes out of their mouths.
It is underneath their cars and in the foundations.

The bathrooms don't say men or women.
Just *Come in and do what you have to do.*

We are eating at a place with *food* in the name.
We get our leftovers to go and

give them to the first person we see who needs it.
Living gallery. Breathing art.

Viva La Gastronomie

The restaurants here have names like
The Satin Doll, Viva Mexico, The Cuban Revolution.
They seem more like situations than places to eat.

We Stumble Into a Free Concert in Water Place Park

Group Love, the crowd shouts the band's name over and over.
We have never heard of them but the thousands of people here

know every word. We need to get out more.
A woman below us is taking pictures with her cell phone.

She puts it away between her tank top and her breast.
I turn to Addie and say, *that's the money shot.*

We are dead center but can't see the band at all.
But the crowd is its own concert. The arms in sync. The jumps.

The band has one request, we make as much noise as possible.
We oblige. The river goes up in flames.

At the Bed and Breakfast's Breakfast

The young couple seated at the two top
(we're at the community table)
looks at the Boston Weather
(there is water in the air)
She is clearly in charge
(isn't that always the way)
Says if we are rained out
she will be the worst person
in the world to be with.
(worse than Hitler?)
I want to ask the man boy
(that's what I call him)
if he has a backup girlfriend
in case this happens.
(it was peach stuffed French toast
by the way)

Trash day in Providence

I don't know why this surprises me.

I Like Being in the Smallest State

It's just my size.

Benefit Street

I
Our tour guide has no eyebrows.
Rhode island is such a small state
there's no room for them.

II
Addie reaches out and caresses my back.
Says *hi*. Says it's too hot to hold hands
But just wanted to touch me. You should all
have an Addie.

III
The Providence Athenaeum, where Edgar Allan Poe visited
Providence's Native Son, has four Brautigan hardbacks.
Makes it worth the hundred dollar annual membership fee.
I'm sure Desmond Tutu flipped through them when he visited.

IV
Our guide tells us in front of the
Rhode Island School of Design Museum
that they have everything from soup to nuts
adding *if you like that kind of thing.*
implying she doesn't like either. I ask her
if the soup is vegetarian. She takes it literally
and tells me *well they do have a cafe.*

V
Our Rhode Island guide
tells *stupid Massachusetts* stories.
It's all they've got.

VI
The rivalry between our guide
and the one in the Stephen Hopkins House
is tangible. Like our guide is Rhode Island
and the other is Massachusetts. Rhode island
wants to tell us all about it. Massachusetts
doesn't give a damn.

VII
I want to say
at the building called
Shakespeare's Head
that this is where they
brought *Shakespeare's head*
when he died.
In fact, I do say it.
Doesn't make it true
though.

Rhode Island School of Design Museum

I
I like the up going down way.

II
We see a giant belly-less Buddha
which would be remarkable if we weren't
already aware of this style of Buddha statue.
So forget I said anything.
(at least it was giant)

III
In The Everyday Things Gallery

Here they make the mundane spectacular.
A watermelon, a paper bag, a garden hose.
I want to lay out all my possessions.
Let onlookers imagine their stories.
Look at this bagel!
This egg sandwich
encased in glass!

IV
A jar of sunflower seeds

Again I get the feeling one of the workers
left this here and they surrounded it with a
display case. I have no problem with this.

V
We see a large wooden bust which could
be a Christ but Addie says his hair is lion-like.
In the next room, a mosaic of an actual lion
which I point to and say *I can't tell
if this is a lion or a Christ.*
This is one of those points
where Addie wants it noted on the record
that she would slap me if she
were the kind of person to do so.

VI
All these ancient Greek fighting scenes
depicted in marble makes me think their civilization
would have lasted longer if they wore clothing when
they were fighting.

VII
The Diners (les soupeurs)
Pablo Picasso, 1901

We see an early more conventional
looking Picasso. Almost impressionistic.
Before he got all crazy and started adding
boobs everywhere.

VIII
A Walk in the Fields at Argenteuil
Claude Monet, 1873

Monet shorthands the year with his signature
'73 - not imagining we would be looking at his paintings
two centuries later.

We are still looking Claude.

IX
The African Venus
Charles Henri Joseph Cordier

We see a black woman
with great hair
standing in front of
a statue of a black woman
with great hair.

She has great hair
Addie remarks.

X
Cyrus and Frank Taft
James Sullivan Lincoln, 1860

We see a painting of
two babies seated with
mature heads which we call
The Man Babies.

XI
I call a dress with a large translucent protrusion
an *ass dress*. I am quickly told by a woman with more
knowledge than me who I happen to be married to that
it is a maternity dress and the protrusion is for the baby bump,
and not, in fact, for the ass.

XII
We leave our water bottles
in the coat room thus
redefining what coat
rooms can be for
generations to come.

WaterFire

haiku

Everything about
Providence is waiting for
the river to burn

I Once Thought This at the Ocean

All I can think of is accidentally dropping my phone into the river. I want to throw it in so I can stop worrying about it.

It's Happened Before

Addie is concerned she might fall in.
I point to the nearest spot where she would
be able to climb up and we're resting easier knowing
at the very least she won't die.

A Difference

A police boat swims by.
Normally they'd arrest people
who try to burn things.

Too Much Thought

Addie is looking for excuses to go back into the restaurant to use their bathroom. We finished eating and left there an hour ago. What is the statute of limitations on such things? I had already gone back in telling them I left my water bottle at the table. I suggest she could go in and tell them she left her urine in her body, which was technically partially generated by the Asian Pear Martini they served us. Before I can fully flesh out this idea she is already on her way with her own plan.

Family

I
A family from the holy land sits next to us by the river.
We are not fluent but can tell when the mother asks
if they want ice cream. She asks in Hebrew. They answer
in English. This is America and they can't risk misunderstanding
where ice cream is concerned.

II
My people are not a quiet people.
One can only hope when the music starts
they will experience a certain reverence.
When the boats with the flames come,
a quiet awe.

Anticipation

This is our second night of music on a river
First the Charles on Independence Day
and now...well I don't even know the name of this river
but there *is* music. The sun is legally down.
The flames are coming.

Life

A crab
Legal Seafood size
swims under our feet.
It's not his first
WaterFire.

Flower Before Fire

They pass out free carnations
To anyone who wants one
They are not part of the ceremony
They just think that people who come to WaterFire
are wonderful. We take a red one.

Nearby a drummer in a boat has a flame.

The River is On Fire

I
Water Place Basin
Koftos from the speakers
red carnation in hand
It is hot - a product of fire.
We are awesome
for being here.

II
Someone said it doesn't make sense
to stay longer than a half hour.
I can't imagine ever leaving.

III
This is the ultimate, a citywide campfire.
We imagine vegan marshmallows.
We'd need a canoe or a really long stick.
We'd like to break out our guitars
but the artist has chosen the soundtrack.

IV
Lovers in gondolas drift by.
I don't know them but who else would
be in a gondola but lovers?

V
Our carnation twists into the river.
Soon everything will be in the river.

VI
I take pictures of the fire
Like I've never seen it before.

VII
Providence is not about
patriots and revolutions.
It is about what is possible when
the muskets have been put away.
It is about this.

VIII
If this weren't all enough
a man twirling fire floats by.

IX
Men with cameras on boats film the fire.
Once the *braziers* extinguish, this fire is gone.

X
The boats come and
the people dressed in black
put more logs in. This night
will go on all night.

After WaterFire

We Want to Put Food in Our Mouths

Addie has decided it is the hot dog part of the night.
But unlike Toronto there are no vegetarian hot dogs in sight.
So it's melted chocolate, a shot of Chambord and things to dip.
The Indians called it fondue and it is part of our sacred heritage.

Punking in Providence

A couple runs across the street
in the opposite direction of us.
I shout to them *hurry up you're missing it*
referring to nothing at all.

We Know This is Wrong

It's amateur night at the fondue place.
Our waiter's first night. They're running
out of fruit and we're seated next to a portable
air conditioning unit. We overhear the waiter
at another table tell his patrons "you don't

go under there." Technically he's right but
what situation has happened to inspire
that to be said out loud? He brings us
our check "just so we would have it."
Does that mean we can keep it?

We don't have to pay? We put the credit
card in the thingy and stick it as far out
over the table as possible. We hope he will
see it someday and we can go home.
Finally he arrives...apologizes...he was cleaning.

We want him to feel good about his first day
and offer jokes about how he'll become sick of fondue.
He says he already is as he started as a busboy
and used to sample the chocolates off the tables
he cleared. This really is too much information.

A couple tables away one busboy tells another
how something was stolen from this exact
table. We leave them to their mystery
hoping for a future fondue experience catering
to experts like us. We head outside where

the fire still burns.

Last Night of Vacation

This bed is too big for
the smallest state.
Requires a ladder.

Sensitivity

They served whipped butter with breakfast.
I wonder if that makes anyone else uncomfortable.

Dénouement

The Last Exit Out of New York is Arthur Kill Road

I'm not sure if

a) Arthur was killed here

b) Arthur killed the road here somehow

c) Arthur is a killer celebrated by this road for some reason

d) This is where one would go to kill someone named Arthur (and if so would you have to bring your own Arthur or would they supply one)

In any case, we have just entered New Jersey where it is not wise to ask questions.

I've Gained Five Pounds on This Trip

Not in body mass, I've just started carrying around a five pound weight out of principle.

My Literacy is Questionable

In a store in Bethlehem, Pennsylvania I see
a book called *Classic Celtic Wisdom* which
I think says *Chasidic Celtic Wisdom*
If only such a thing existed.

Quackvolution

Another store in Bethlehem offers
a variety of rubber ducks. They say
A duck for every stage of life.
Finally a method of marking the
milestones of my journey
that makes sense.

In Front of the Moravian

A rain drop just fell in my eye.
At least I hope it's rain and not
someone spitting off the roof
of the oldest bookstore in the
United States.

Tired

It is our last day
in bed in Allentown.
There is no more research to be done.
No more details to add to the itinerary.
From this point it is only
the airport and airport food
and airplane windows and
a descent through smog and
an assortment of ground transportation and
a late night unlocking of a door and
a pile of mail and
relieved cats and
a frog who doesn't know
the difference and
a familiar bed and
a sleep
a long
long sleep.

Spiritual

This plane
is bound for L.A.
this plane.

By the Time You Read This Book Our Son Probably Still Won't Be Potty Trained

We've been rewarding our son with toys
when he's used the potty so when he runs up
to the strangers at the airport, holds up
his Spiderman motorcycle and says
I got this because I pooped!
it was, Indeed, a reward for all.

Later he asks another three year old
if he can drive the motorcycle on her head.
She says *yes,* out of professional courtesy.

The author, presumptuously posed at the Museum of Fine Arts, Boston

About The Author

Rick Lupert has been involved in the Los Angeles poetry community since 1990. He served for two years as a co-director of the Valley Contemporary Poets, a non-profit organization which produces readings and publications out of the San Fernando Valley. His poetry has appeared in numerous magazines and literary journals, including The Los Angeles Times, Rattle, Chiron Review, Red Fez, Zuzu's Petals, Stirring, The Bicycle Review, Caffeine Magazine, Blue Satellite and others. He edited the anthologies Ekphrastia Gone Wild - Poems Inspired by Art, A Poet's Haggadah: Passover through the Eyes of Poets, and The Night Goes on All Night - Noir Inspired Poetry, and is the author of fourteen other books: Death of a Mauve Bat, Sinzibuckwud!, We Put Things In Our Mouths, Paris: It's The Cheese, I Am My Own Orange County, Mowing Fargo, I'm a Jew. Are You?, Feeding Holy Cats, Stolen Mummies, I'd Like to Bake Your Goods, A Man With No Teeth Serves Us Breakfast (Ain't Got No Press), Lizard King of the Laundromat, Brendan Constantine is My Kind of Town (Inevitable Press) and Up Liberty's Skirt (Cassowary Press). He has hosted the long running Cobalt Café reading series in Canoga Park since 1994 and is regularly featured at venues throughout Southern California.

Rick created and maintains the Poetry Super Highway, an online resource and publication for poets. (PoetrySuperHighway.com)

Currently Rick works as a music teacher at synagogues in Southern California and as a graphic and web designer for anyone who would like to help pay his mortgage.

Rick's Other Books

Death of a Mauve Bat
Ain't Got No Press ~ January, 2012

The Night Goes On All Night
Noir Inspired Poetry (edited by)
Ain't Got No Press ~ November, 2011

Sinzibuckwud!
Ain't Got No Press ~ January, 2011

We Put Things In Our Mouths
Ain't Got No Press ~ January, 2010

A Poet's Haggadah (edited by)
Ain't Got No Press ~ April, 2008

A Man With No Teeth Serves Us Breakfast
Ain't Got No Press ~ May, 2007

I'd Like to Bake Your Goods
Ain't Got No Press ~ January, 2006

Stolen Mummies
Ain't Got No Press ~ February, 2003

Brendan Constantine is My Kind of Town
Inevitable Press ~ September, 2001

Up Liberty's Skirt
Cassowary Press ~ March, 2001

Feeding Holy Cats
Cassowary Press ~ May, 2000

I'm a Jew, Are You?
Cassowary Press ~ May, 2000

Mowing Fargo
Sacred Beverage Press ~ December, 1998

Lizard King of the Laundromat
The Inevitable Press ~ February, 1998

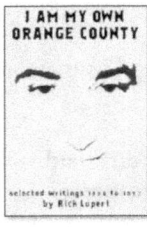 

I Am My Own Orange County
Ain't Got No Press ~ May, 1997

Paris: It's The Cheese
Ain't Got No Press ~ May, 1996

For more information:
http://PoetrySuperHighway.com/

www.ingramcontent.com/pod-product-compliance
Lightning Source LLC
LaVergne TN
LVHW051052080426
835508LV00019B/1826